THE IRON BRIDGE

Rebecca Hurst is a writer, opera-maker, and illustrator based in Greater Manchester. Her poetry has appeared in various magazines and anthologies, including Carcanet's *New Poetries VIII*. She is the author of a poetry pamphlet, *The Fox's Wedding* (The Emma Press, 2022). Rebecca has a PhD from the University of Manchester, and is co-founder of the Voicings Collective, an ensemble that devises new music theatre. She teaches creative writing in hospitals, schools, universities, museums and the community.

The Iron Bridge

Rebecca Hurst

CARCANET POETRY

First published in Great Britain in 2024 by
Carcanet
Alliance House, 30 Cross Street
Manchester, M2 7AQ
www.carcanet.co.uk

A CIP catalogue record for this book is
available from the British Library.

ISBN 978 1 80017 394 1

Book design by Andrew Latimer, Carcanet
Typesetting by LiteBook Prepress Services
Printed in Great Britain by SRP Ltd, Exeter, Devon

MIX
Paper from
responsible sources
FSC   FSC® C014540
www.fsc.org

The publisher acknowledges financial
assistance from Arts Council England.

Supported using public funding by
ARTS COUNCIL
ENGLAND

CONTENTS

III: NIGHT JOURNEYS

IV: AN EXPLORER'S HANDBOOK

For Luka

The secret is to walk evading nothing
through rain sleet darkness wind,
not to abandon the spirit of repetition:
— ALICE OSWALD

What we habitually see confirms us.
— JOHN BERGER

THE IRON BRIDGE

ROUGH MUSIC

Eye-level with the blacksmith's bench, his daughter
picks through the mess of nails and bolts to find,
clean amongst the grease, a silver gleam.

The ball-bearings flash from her fingers,
skitter, comet-bright, across the concrete floor.
She scrambles after the little balls of light

until the chase becomes a game, a race from
forge to yard, as laughter cracks the grip
of her father's craft, the striking and shaping.

To silence her the blacksmith hurls
a hammer. It does not reach its target,
the daughter he dashes after –

down the garden, his face an anvil. Still
she remembers how she jumped into the lilacs
to escape. How his hand reached through

the blooms and grabbed the roots of her hair.
How she rolled up in the dirt like a woodlouse.
How she turned into a pillar of salt, hands

clamped over ears and eyes squeezed tight
to deflect whatever loud, bad thing
was coming: the furnace-red gape.

She remembers late that same day she sat and
held his rough hands. Each nail a half-moon
of dirt; his knuckles scarred, callused, burned.

After any job he did there was some tiny piece left over.
Like a poem, with words that rub and won't sit flush.
The acrid stink of coal smoke makes her sick. No blacksmith

can bear a world without forge, anvil or furnace.
Without fire and quenching water. Here she stands –
his untempered daughter. The one who holds a pen,

who's loyal, who has inherited her father's quick temper
and rough hands. When she hears a hammer dropped
on concrete it chimes like his voice calling.

I: MAPPING THE WOODS

This wood has a thousand exits and entrances:
stiles, gates and tripets, gaps and breaches.

This wood is hammer-pond, clay and chalybeate,
charcoal and slag heaps, leats and races.

This wood hides the boar in a thickety hemmel;
is home to flindermouse, scutty, and kine.

This wood is cut and coppiced and burned;
chestnut and hazel broom-handles turned.

This wood is two green flanks of sandstone
pinched by the link of iron bridge over water.

This wood holds its secrets: the peat-black
knuckerhole where the dragon sleeps.

This wood scolds with a tawny owl's brogue
shrucking and shraping, kewick hoohoo.

This wood is ashen, eldern, and oaken –
a mile from the village, ring-fenced, well-trodden.

Daybreak. This wood calls you out of your house
to walk through leaf-fall and bluebells and moss.

[East Sussex, May 2009]

PENTECOST

At season's height it comes over us like a green flame
snouting the air for summer's imminence; cloven tongues

greening so thickly they must be harvested with scythes.
We fill barns and kitchens with crates of the verdant spears.

You tell me it is called Hadley Grass because it greens
with exuberance in fields along the Connecticut river valley.

It is the acid green of all sprouting things charged to break
winter's spell. As the snow clears and soil warms – up it roars.

It holds winter in its green stem – thick as a man's thumb. It does not bow
to the wind or hail. It drinks rain like a dog sucking water from a puddle.

Its green bounty cannot be contained, though we try: poaching,
pickling, canning, roasting, even churning it into ice cream.

We eat a scoop in waffle cones while sitting on the front porch.
The ice cream is a frosted green and tastes both vegetable and not.

We stare across the fields to where above Mount Tom's slow-greening flank
there is a cindery bank of clouds. We talk in fits and starts. Fall quiet.

The ice cream melts on our green tongues. We watch the moon, gold as the yolk
of a poached egg, push up through the clouds and sail clear of the hill.

[Hadley, Massachusetts, May 2018]

DARK PEAK

It's two years since I've been
to the hills. Winter, spring –
tethered to the valley floor I watch them
hunch down. Slowly, when I can, I hobble
along the rutted track that falls due east
from the Saxon church on the ridge towards
(if I could go) Kinder Scout's flat, notched
crown. I tell them, *I'm waiting.* They shrug.
Indifference is trout-brown, ash-green. Summer
comes. Language rushes through me like rain-
water through gritstone. This gap in the wall
is as far as I can go today. Tomorrow. I stand
in the shade of a hornbeam to sketch the summit.
The rough line bumps against the edge of the page
so I turn and let it wander verso from right to left.
On the wall my fingertips read the fine grain, sickle-
sharp; old news that I carry with me on the walk home.
Somedays wind carries word of the hills; smoke from
moorland fires pricks the air. The rivers Goyt and
Etherow – which at their confluence swirl back
against each other – exchange gossip; clamour;
I stand on the bank and listen to their talk of fitful
rain, drought, cloudbursts and diversions during which
they probe loose soil, slate tiles, red brick, barrow bones
and bling, porcelain chips, a blue glass bead. All the news
from the hills these past one thousand years. Today I linger,
listen to them speak of their work making, reshaping.
We've had a night of heavy rain. The silty waters
roar in spate. Trout-brown, ash-green –
a process like any other – they
carry the hills to the sea.

[Mellor, July 2020]

DESIRE LINES

Facing the glass, lamplight divulges the lines silvering skin between
throat and breast. These days what I want is straightforward:
my daughter's good health; a decent night's sleep; to walk land
that sparks my senses like fire flies netting the summer night.

Sleepless I set to the task of recreating in mind a walk to Parson's Wood,
across the iron bridge and back home down the High Street at dusk, as shops
are closing. The wood brinks on a southern ridge. A creased line of oak and
beech. Paths among the trees converge, pushing eagerly through a gap

in the hedge until one day – a fence, wire between hazel stakes diverts
the path which steps back on either side, affronted. I split the line
with wire-cutters and leave it neatly folded, this path being an expression
of my longing: a way through the dirt and grass, ribwort and cinquefoil

to last a season. More if my desire chimes with others' restlessness: as feet
press down blades of grass, trample and score movement, compact the earth
across lawns, verges, playing fields, public places: as we circumnavigate
or trace each other's paths, and our feet inscribe their lines of yearning.

[East Sussex, June 2016]

Parson's Wood, Mayfield, East Sussex
Longitude: 51.061001
Latitude: 0.308827

[...] woods are evidently places propitious for wandering, or
getting lost in, all woods are a sort of labyrinth.
(Francis Ponge, *The Notebook of the Pine Woods.*)

I. Winter solstice

(21 December 2009
sunrise: 08.00 am
sunset: 03.54 pm)

Between dark and dusk
we walk to the brink of the year,
an iron-red line on cinereous clay.

Hands cramp with cold on the old road
as we sketch and note this half hour
past sunrise but not brightening
though the rooks are awake and jigging
on the frosted shoulders of a broad oak.

Pass a nip of brandy, roll another smoke.
Make a mark
                    and a mark   on the damp page.

This winter's day the wood is a room,
screened by snow, shuttered and barred,
                              nothing doing.

Yes, we feel the Parson's coppiced acres,
feel the chalybeate and charcoal in our bones.

Three walkers, we beat the bounds,
talking of other pilgrimages:
the vixen's path
                    the vole's path
                              the roebuck's.

From the knap of this hill the wood
is perspicuous. It holds a pose:
the line of golden larches, the net
of branches the beech casts to the sky.

Count the ways in:
the tracks and driftways,
sheere-ways and bostals,
gaps, twittens and stiles.

Loop round and back again.
These Wealden hills burn us up –
the effort of taking them in snow.

Fumbling in pockets for a pencil stub
I trace the shape of a chestnut bole,
a rosette of reindeer moss.
The doctor's lanky son peers down,
says, '*Cla-cla-donia rangiferina*,'
and harrups to clear his throat.
Rolls another smoke.
Siân hands out gold chocolate coins,
blows her cold-pinked nose.

By the hammer pond we peer
through the burne-washed brick tunnel.
The water races, black as slate.
Three centuries back there was a foundry
here: a pond bay, trough and furnace.
We light a cardboard waterwheel.
It doubles, spins and crackles.
The old year creaks, then turns
as with a flash the flames ignite
quick as the robin flits
across the ice-fringed pool.

Night comes early.
We set a candle in the window.
There is stew in the oven,
wine, bread and salt on the table.
Johnny draws back the curtains
and St George ambles
through the unlocked door.
We cheer as he slays the Turk
with his righteous sword,
cheer louder when the dead man
is magicked back to life.

Walking home through the wood
an hour past midnight
I find a chestnut leaf
      lying on the path
                fallen
picked up
             then palmed

between the pages of this notebook.

II. Spring equinox

(20 March 2010
sunrise: 06.03 am
sunset: 06.10 pm)

Sugar moon, stiff hands flexing.
Station Street to High Street
down Fletching Street to Coggin's Mill.
The air is tepid and thick.
Mist draws down along
the sandstone ridge.
Traffic reporting from the A26.
Birdsong quadraphonic,
simulcasting spring.
I feel it too.
Yawn, warming
as I walk, and
my body yields.

At Johnny's house a bedroom window
is propped open. We shout in the dark,
'Wake up lapsy!' and a lean shadow
calls, 'Good morning! Be right down.'
We take a thermos of tea, fill our pockets
with Simnel cake and tie our bootlaces tight.

6.04 am. A minute past the day's dawning
but no sun. Just grey cloud and the clatter
of the burne, rain-choked and precipitate.

We circle the rough-sketched
woodland, walking in silence.

Downstream from the hammer pond
we paddle along a reach of gravel.
Above us the bank rises ten feet sheer.
We dig in the clay for nuggets
of charcoal, slag and ore,
grubbing out a lump of iron
big as my head. It is cast
with foliage, a dainty kissing ball
made of lion's mouth, celandine,
hemlock and stitchwort.

Later we sit in a row on a gate
and Johnny tells a story
he heard from Alf Clout –
'There was a white bullock
round as the moon
who broke a fence
and lost himself deep
in this tangled thicket.
He dwells here still,
and each year in March
there's one who will see him.
And they're in for a hard year,
poor soul, for a glimpse
of the white stot bodes ill.'

We nod, make note and eat our sandwiches.

Twelve hours pass in doing
                                    not much

but walking and watching the shift
in shade and tone on this sunless day.

We wash our hands and drink from the spring,
tie three-dozen ribbons to the ash tree
that sprouts nearby;
a wish for every
bright strip of cloth
binding us close
to this crooked place.

The flat light drains colour from the fields,
submerges the intricacies of the wood
and exhausts the gaze. Nightfall
revives the faded landscape
just as it begins to rain
and we see the gleaming bones
of a long-dead oak and the bronze
and mauve of budding trees.

Still walking, homeward now, heads down
against the rain, ready to see this bout through,
we cover the conifer plantation
make our last lap along the Little Rother.

Mud licks our boots. We walk blind
night-fallen, surefooted. Until
the path dips and there is a flurry
like a leaf turning in the breeze.
Siân stops.
        Peers down.
'A toad,' she calls out in warning
                and summoning
for then there is a frog and a frog
                and another toad
and five, six, seven more
                leaping up from beneath our feet
green and gold on grey.

We walk single file
heads bowed
and counting
our steps
with care
on this most lively
road through the woods
knowing
they've woken
to warmth and dark
and wriggled
from their muddy holes
to mate in the puddles and ponds
where they were spawned.

We hear them
        crooning now –
for this damp gloaming is
        their unimaginable
high noon
        and the wet
and the warmth
        and the woods
have called
        and they have come.

III. Summer solstice

(21 June 2010
sunrise: 04.44 am
sunset: 09.17 pm)

Milk thistle is the solitary maid
settling her spindle in the coppice
amongst the chestnut boles
and bee-fingered foxgloves.

The stream is silent, stretching
itself from blue sunrise to last light,
seventeen hours long. No rush then.

And the leaf canopy is a bold new green,
while fireweed and knapweed,
ragwort and buttercup scald
the fields and verges and tracts
of common ground.

We follow a fox-track flush
with orchids and milk-maids,
make tea from pods of Solomon's seal,
inhale the rare steam and lie about
in the long grass waiting
and reading aloud.

Johnny unpacks the picnic:
bread, cheese, tomatoes
red as my sun-flushed face,
Milton's *Comus*,
a dish of watercress,
another of strawberries.

Taking off his shirt and tilting his hat,
the doctor's son begins to read:

> *The first Scene discovers a wild wood.*
> *The* ATTENDANT SPIRIT *descends or enters.*

Afternoon dozing –

> (I dream of a woman
> sitting with her lap full
> of some puzzle of yarn.
> She wears green and gold
> and is all pins and needles,
> bobbins, hooks and barbs.
>
> She reaches out and snips
> a slit in the day with tiny brass scissors.
> The sun slides through the tear…)

And wake to see the runic heron
tow its long legs across the sky.
Rooks follow, black ribbons
unspooling.

        It is time then
and we take tea-lights
to the hammer pond
while night seeps in
                  like a promise half-kept
and we light the dish of black water.

Now this small place
is an amphitheatre,
the stories we tell in whispers, epic.

Siân spins a yarn:

The way she tells it
the scraggly milk thistle
moves at night
on tattered feet. I believe
she has that in her,
to tear herself from the soil,
                    to creep
close,
        closer.

And at daybreak to replant her feet
in charcoal and clay,
far from home
and back again.

IV. Autumn equinox

>   (23 September 2010
>   sunrise: 06.47 am
>   sunset: 06. 57 pm)

The rosebay willowherb
has gone to spume.
Siân, leading the way,
finds a great web
blocks our path.
The spider – a stripy-legged man –
hovers in the corner of his larder-loom.

We have been out for an hour.
The birds are rousing.
My stomach growls.
I pick blackberries.
A hazel leaf shivers
                and drops.

This wood was full of children
when I was young.
We built dens using cut branches
the men who came to coppice
left behind. And in charcoal pits
lit fires, cooked our tea –
cans of beans and sausages.
We came here with matches
and small dogs, homemade
bows and arrows
and paper boats
and penny chews.
We skinny-dipped
in the hammer pond,
stayed out too late,
let the glow-worms
light us home.

I knew all the old stories:
dragons and devils,
saints and smiths,
tusked wild boar,
the white bull lost
and still looking
for a way through.

At night sometimes
tucked up in bed
I heard him roar.

And yet for all that
the wood let us enter
and saw us leave
to live our lives,
grow up,
move away.

Now I think on it
there were only three of us
playing in the wood.
Sister, friend, and me.
Now three again
constructing a sukkah
of willow and bracken.
Lying inside we look up –
see the tawny autumn
leaves and the blue sky.

Later I sit on an oak limb
shaggy with lichen.
The air is warm
on my bare arms.
I feel just right,
                    at home
here in my skin
and in the woods,
up to my ankles
in leaf-mould
and sphagnum moss.

Beyond
the clamour of insects
rises in waves and rolls down
the sun-struck meadow.
The shrilling fills the wood
like a hive brewing to swarm.

And yes, I hear you calling.
I take off my shoes.
Remember we said
we'd walk home barefoot?
The ground is warm
and turning.

And a week still to go. Days of drizzle and midges.
The croft, cramped and low, good to walk from.
The grown-ups' wan interest in all but ferry times,
tides, and the opening hours of the pub in Oban.

And aged five or six, unwatched for the first time,
following a sheep track down past the black broch,
its dome cracked, to the place where land rears back
from the sea. Beyond the trough of waves are mountains.

I stand, an astonished body, north-struck, eyes glamoured
by light on water, sea and sky supple as sealskin,
rocks sunk to their chins in lichen and moss, waves fretting
against the bare shelves of mica-spackled granite.

I stand on the shore amid rafts of wrack and dulse,
gravel lax beneath my feet and water soft as driftwood.
Beyond the surf's complicating lacework, stranded
on a sheet of grey sand, a jelly-fish: *Aurelia aurita.*

And I see – the moon deflated; a collapsed umbrella;
an eye reflecting the sky's astonishment and its own
domed-self. I squat down on the sand to look closer
at the gelatinous saucer, count 1-2-3-4 lilac rings.

And that night, bathing in peat-gold water, I trawl
with my flannel. The nubby cloth blooms and pulses,
summoning the jelly-fish – wave locked within wave –
lobbed into an element previously unimagined, struck

by the weight of gravity's suck on its tulle skirts and
tentacle ribbons. On yielding, lying slack, aware or not
of the surf retreating, opaquely eyeing the mackerel sky
and the child who has come to find it.

[Scotland, August 1976]

LLYN DDU/BLACK LAKE/LINDOW

August. And the country enchanted – locked in drought.
Parking outside the nature reserve's gate I walk through
shield fern and bushy, new-growth birch, onto Lindow Moss.

My plan, to walk an hour or two over this erstwhile bog; a pit
from which black peat has been extracted leaving a flat pan
of tawny dirt; twisted, discarded boles and branches; black-

water stagnating in drainage ditches. I sit on a sun-bleached
trunk. A fly begs to tell me all the secrets of this place if only
I'll let it settle in my ear. I sit and wait for the bog to fold

me under, watching not just the remorseless carousel of planes
that rise / fall beyond the trees one after another. Not just the lone
rabbit's white scut. But a circle of tufted bog cotton, the glint

of peat-stained water, iron spade, crisp packet, tobacco pouch,
moss-packed milk bottle, cinquefoil, and at my feet ash-pale
ground streaked black. I scratch the dirt to discover not charcoal

or spilled oil, but damp seeping up from deep under. A place
half-remembering itself as spring, bog, pool, llyn and mere;
the formation of a sphagnum raft floating over open water.

Later, walking back to the car, I spot a plump, tarnished green
scrap of moss. Despite the drought, blazing sun, and stripped-bare
ground something has felt the urge to start over. *Bryum argenteum*:

a species of wasteland, stone walls, slate roofs, gathering dust
in its feathered tufts to extend its growth. Silvery thread moss
willing to let down tender fibrils. To feel that here is enough.

[Cheshire, August 2022]

BRIDGEWATER

After tea, a break in the rain. We go back to the city
at 4 miles/hour: walking pace: pace of conversation
to the engine's thumping metronome. Ed, bundled up,
steers us between mudbank and towpath, through

sunset, twilight, nightfall, in quick succession.
The beam of the tunnel-lamp illuminates now
the hawthorn hedge, frost-glamoured; now
the tall concrete arch of the M60 ring-road

and we're back amongst warehouses and brick mills.
Near midnight on the shortest day of the year
we cruise into Castlefield; cluster of glass towers
and steel cranes, red lights winking like baubles.

Maybe it's the rhubarb gin, or the candlelight
and flare of the fire, or the barely-there-sway
of the boat as I sit on the steps by the stove, face
too hot, my back to an open door and the cold.

We go outside and stand on the prow. Wave back
to Ed. Coal-smoke pricks the air. You might ask
(but won't) what lies beneath the black water
alongside shopping trolleys and bike frames

ransacked handbags and hen-night inflatables.
Your head is on my shoulder and we slip out
of the flow of mother, daughter, carried down
away into the uncontainable and rough-hewn past –

a trough long as the canal basin, hand-dug
250 years ago by men whose labour, sweat, curses
are long gone beneath the murk; the homes and land
they left; the songs they sang to fuel their graft.

What lies behind is sunk. All that's left is midnight,
diesel fumes, the engine's cough as it stops. Ed calls
out and you take the coil of rope, jump across the reach
of black water and make fast the narrow boat.

[Manchester, December 2018]

THE LAND

Somewhere just south of here, a woman whose DNA
I hold in my bones was born, lived, died: a field worker.
What that meant I can imagine (barely) having worked
on farms myself until I figured out another way. Or rather
until my body wasn't having any. Even now, the knot
of pinched nerves in my lower back is giving me stick.

Four hours from Manchester and I skim the flat
depleted farmlands of Nottinghamshire, Lincolnshire,
soaring into Norfolk on A-roads bedecked by last year's
broccoli, bolted and blowsy along the verge.
I too am making an unseasonable foray, from cityscape
to fields of blue cabbage and an acid-spill of daffodils.

In the distance bulky figures wade through the flowers,
stooping to cut them close to the ground. One stands, flexes
sap-sodden fingers, turns to face the sun, bends back down.
On a roundabout near Swaffham I pass a turnip, thunderous
and churly, in the outside lane. Pass a convoy of lorries parked up
beside a mountain of beet. Pass over a river; the Great Ouse.

Fens, dykes, drained marshland, land for sale, developed, chainlink-
fenced, McDonalds one after another, counting down the miles
to being with you again and noticing through a shower of hail
and rain: each green blade, cloud, new leaf. Late-afternoon I reach
St Margaret of Antioch's. You're waiting there for me. The land
fades with the light and from the churchyard we can hear the sea.

[Norfolk, February 2020]

BANKSY WOOD

It could be a metaphor, but for now it's a just place, raw as a
skinned knee.
A tangle of larch, holly, and beech. Banks of slag, clay,
sandstone. A stream.

The wood floor is anvil-hard. Gone: bluebell bulbs, litter-fall,
mycelium's soft web.
Almost obscene, how rain hammers thin, acidic soil; lays bald
the sandstone.

Gone: chewy mounds of moss, hart's tongue, clumps of hard
fern, bracken,
walks-past. Licked clean by Baba Yaga's broom. Swept
downhill to the stream.

We skitter through. Twigs scoot loose underfoot. No pur-
chase on this detritus.
Flotsam not settled to the quiet business of rot-down into
clay and sandstone.

Folding ourselves under toppled trees we circumnavigate an
old hawthorn.
Untethered, it floats where a path used to follow the drift
down to the stream.

Gone: all trace of old ways, no clarity 'til swinging birch to
birch we glide the last
slick reach to iron bridge. Below, water shudders, silty with
clay, sandstone.

I let you walk on ahead as I peer down into trash-clogged
    water. The wood I knew
has been churned away like this branch of hawthorn washed
    down to the stream —

a branch still green in leaf, yet red and heavy with haws, torn
    from a living tree and
swept through fields farms villages past steep banks of grey
    clay, gold sandstone

to where stream meets river and the tribute it carries is em-
    braced by a grate
that diverts the flood. Yes, wood and paths are gone, but the
    stream roars on.

[East Sussex, September 2021]

WONE

The iron bridge stands its ground
gathering land to water across
thin air. The drop, nine foot
on either side, holds gusts of midges
and looping light from the sandstone
bank. Early evening. The western sky
is charcoal foxed with gold. The bridge
does not dwell. No more do I and
each time it is harder to return. But
the bridge – I think it knows me
even after five years gone. My heel
strikes a spark, iron on flint
and the bridge recalls the press
of my hand on the cold rail and
the point I stop, always, and turn
to look downstream, to see the way
water shivers across a shallow reach
of gravel. Yes, the bridge is a thing
of this sort, spanning water with iron
and concrete to lift me through air
and make a place to hesitate and turn
to look downstream, feel again the rub
of the stranger's child, that familiar nudge
as the mind unmoors and pours
out of my mouth and eyes and ears

And this moment on the iron bridge quiets
my eye, and place and time converge and
are nested like a yolk inside its shell.
The bridge straddles more than
half my life, stepping wide across
the murmuring stream. It is a charm
against fretful darkness. It is the thing
I set my mind towards when I step over
the threshold, cross the churchyard and
down the gully into Parson's Wood.
When I set my feet in the direction
of the bridge I am already there
hand resting on cold iron rail
turning to look downstream,
as I could not carry myself across
the bridge if I had not first imagined
reaching it in my mind. For I am here,
stuck in this everyday body at my desk,
and again climbing over the stile as I write
the coppiced wood, then one foot on clay
and one foot on concrete stepping forward,
already there in mind, hesitating at the
halfway point, standing as I will always do
to look downstream   and only in this way
can I cross the iron bridge

[East Sussex, 13 October 2015]

II: THE STRANGER'S CHILD

HIDE & SEEK

She chased them all – St Stephen's freckled wren,
the Whitsun Man, John Barleycorn and his bride –
from first frost to leaf-fall, from old moon to cold.

Now it is Michaelmas: the land sun-warm,
fields shorn, blackberries ripe to bursting.
And on she quests, hide and seeker, bow-tuned

and wearing a rank waxed jacket, blunt nose
lifted to the swallocky air. Barefoot past Rusher's,
Hawksden and Sharnden, then down the hollow roads

checking her traps of wire and ribbon.
At dusk she found him mired in heavy clay
– the King of Wands.

He was at bay and panting hard. She branded him.
Burnt her mark in the fist of flesh above his heart
then slashed the snare that held him fast.

He shuddered at her touch, leapt through a gap
in the hedge. Fled. The stream clamoured.
The greenwoods shrugged into nightfall.

A mile away and the white stag stopped to graze
on the flank of a hill, bowed his head
and a blackbird called for rain.

TEETH

Forget her fast. Eyes shut
and split, five, six. Little bitch
little squit. Lost in the woods.
Slam and bolt the door on her.

Pour her away. A saucer
of sour milk. Little stinker
onto the shovel with her.
Spilt. Blink. Lose her quick.

And let the seasons pleat
folding one year to the next
linen stacked in the press.
Stamp the sparks down and still

stories smoulder. Neighbours,
a childless hunter and his wife
thought they saw her
scamper through the trees.

It was mid-winter.
No one in the village
had fuel or food to spare
so they tried to forget her.

But like the keening
of dogs at night
her memory nipped
and snagged their sleep.

It was a thorn caught in the
soft edges of their hard days:
a child alone and trapped
in the snow-shuttered woods.

On the eve of Epiphany
they found her sleeping
in a nest of ice and leaves.
The trees bristled with hoar-frost.

A pack of dogs protected her,
snarling and barking,
lured away by the gift
of raw red meat.

And the hunter carried her
home. Filthy, naked, mute.
They took her in, little cuckoo.
Fed her, dressed her, taught her.

Months passed and the girl learned
the bones of polite behaviour.
Soon she could thread a needle,
sweep the floor, collect the eggs.

She spoke   stammering.
Named things like a spiky
Lilith pointing to
   – this?   – this?   – this?

Again and the mask slipped.
She bared her teeth
snapped at strangers. Bit
striking hard and deep.

Three times she ran to the woods.
Three times the hunter tracked her,
fought off the dogs, caught her,
brought her home.

'Til one fine summer's day
a newspaper man,
just passing through,
saw the story in her.

He photographed her
capering on all fours,
lapping from a dish
laid on the floor. And

the hunter and his wife
let her go. Hoping
to be done with the trouble
and strangeness of her.

Nearly forgot her until
one frost-furred night
they woke to howling
and stood at their window.

Saw her scamper through the trees;
heard her calling, calling.
And heard the wild dogs
in the woods answer her call.

Yes, she barked and howled
with an ease she'd never
coaxed from her human voice.
For like burrs in her matted hair

they had snagged:
the woods, the pack of dogs.
And she had worked her way back
with sharp teeth and claws.

The hunter and his wife heard
their doomed hens squawk
and cry out in warning –
but ran too late to save them.

Found a flurry
of blood
torn feathers
and the girl gone

just the brass latch
on the henhouse door
spun around past
the point of holding.

THE UNRELIABLE NARRATOR

Not a field,
a forest.

Not a key,
a hammer.

Not a sword,
a spindle.

Not a chair,
a ladder.

She barks
like a vixen
sparring with shadows
in the midnight garden.

No guide
she leaves you
on the mountain pass
to wake in the precinct
at dawn
in a nest of newsprint
while around you
schoolchildren
rowdy as rooks
gossip, smoke, spar.

If there is truth
in her
she has yet to find
its edge.

Still, when she gives you
a sprig of larkspur
or a glass of tea
take it.

The amber leaves
blossom as they steep.
The glass sings.
Take a scalding sip.

FIRE SONG

In the Rumble Club the band is setting up: three boys, a drum kit, two guitars and a cat's cradle of electric cords. My sister sits alone at a table under the disco ball. Her pillar-box hair smarts in the wefty black of this music box. People drift in off the street. The tower of amps is fizzing. My sister sits and smokes. The ball begins to spin and silver sparks across her milk-pale face. We wait to hear her sing.

(In the back of the 252 bus my sister holds her lit cigarette against the seat. There is a sizzle, a thread of smoke, and the little black hole winks.)

When she sings she shuts her eyes and touches her red mouth to the mic.

And then there was the time she read my diary. And the time I photographed her lying in a bathtub full of autumn leaves. And the time I climbed a tree to escape the needle-sharp of her voice. And the time we mustered the fireguard and clotheshorse and made a den in the inglenook. Gathered close by the grate we played Robber Princess as the fire scorched our faces, until I found one loose brick in the fireback, hot to the hand and singed black, wobbling like my front tooth. I niggled it free and we pressed our faces to the gap. Beyond there was a strange room – not of our home – with vine-shuttered windows, arsenic green leaves patterning the wallpaper, and a gust of air seasoned with damp, vinegar, and an old churchy fragrance that made our eyes tear. A woman sat an upright piano, her back to us, head bowed, and striking one key / E ♭ / hard, over and again with her index finger. She did not turn but when she spoke we almost remembered her needle-sharp voice: the flare of language. The hot, bad song. 'I know you,' she said. 'I know you. And I know everything about you.'

HOW THE FOX LOST HIS BRUSH

Why do poets invoke the Muse?

(Robert Graves, *The White Goddess.*)

I. Help Wanted

A job with lots of advantages: cosy working conditions, minimal obligations. Required: typing speed of 80 wpm; a sparkling glance; steadfast demeanour. Preferred: able to brew a reviving cup of tea and cook a soft omelette. Occasional evening shift bivouacked under the stars. Therefore good circulation and night vision helpful. Pay commensurate with experience. Room and board provided. Include full-length photograph, dress, and shoe size with application.

II. Appraisal

You were not what I expected (leaf-green girl, first glance, playful pursuit). Instead – a woman that sharp I cut my tongue on her. I was wrong-footed from the moment you accosted me in Woolworths. I: shopping for decongestants (springtime, sinus trouble). You: holding a box of knee-high pop socks and my 'help wanted' ad. I tried, with courtesy, to brush you off, assuming it would not be difficult given your advanced years and limited mobility. But that night as I dined alone in The Original Third Eye, you returned at the very moment I crushed a cardamom pod between my back molars, splitting open the roof of my senses. I gulped Cobra to wash you away but the channels were open and you poured through, clamouring like a lusty sixteen-year-old charging up Crowborough Hill on

Saturday night. There was no tuning you out, no turning you off. I heard you and you doubled down. Then split my lip like some street-brawling slut. I kicked your shins as you clung to me, and woke the next morning bruised from foot to knee, head throbbing, aware that something vital was missing. One week later and you remain camped on my front lawn with your eight shambolic sisters, who blight Rannoch Road with bonfires and bawdy sing-alongs. I sit stuck inside with the curtains drawn. While you squat on my doorstep, your ruined mouth pressed to the letterbox, calling out my name.

SINGING TOGETHER

A morning daffodil bright and she sits, packed with all the rest on narrow benches, singing. Outside the window, beyond the shrill of voices, Harry pushes a mower in circles, laying siege to the ilex tree. *I'll sing you one, O/And green grow the rushes, O.* She presses her knees together against the sharp buzz of love; like growing pains to have her spacious brain suddenly crowded with this someone – his sweet smile and eyes faded blue as his handyman's overalls. At lunchtime she seeks him out against the rules; finds him in the boy's cloakroom. Harry is sloshing a mop around the empty stalls. The rows of duffle coats smack of playground games. Pairs of black plimsolls nest like swallows in their wire cages. She lingers by the door and chats. She likes the way Harry lays down his mop to listen; how his hands hang from knobby wrists; how he chuckles at her tall tales. Later, he is called to the classroom to remove a bumble bee. Standing in the thicket of knee-high desks he is a giant; she knows him from fairy tales. He carries the bee away as if it were a fallen star.

Later, home and watching *Jackanory*, she writes a note using her father's fountain pen. The ink leaves a black spot on her index finger. She signs the note with an flowery *H*, and sleeps with it under her pillow. Now, folded small, the note sits for days in her coat pocket. It is a razor blade. It slits open the seams. It falls to the ground and her mother finds it, unfolds it, reads the careful cursive: *I love you.* Holds the note between thumb and forefinger and says, 'Tell the truth.' Says, 'No one will be angry.' School, the next day, and Mother Superior's voice is a hammer, 'Admit you wrote it yourself. It is your handwriting.'/'It is not!'/'These are your words!'/'They are not!' She watches a column of dust rise and fall in the sunlight.

The window is cracked. From the room below her class singing. *What is your one, O?/One is one and all alone/And evermore shall be so.* And in the distance, the sound of a mower. She says, 'He wrote it. He wrote it!' Her fingers curl fierce-tight around the fib, that nips like a bee sting, a sharp buzz of love. *And green grow the rushes O.*

THE ANIMAL BRIDEGROOM

They say, the Bride wore green and processed
down the narrow, muddy lane in the midst
of a little band – bride and groom, guests with
flags and bunting, drums and horns and bells.
One amongst them summoned a gust of wind.
And a shower blew through, sunshine and rain
a warning that set the mothers running to bring
their children in from play lest they catch
a glimpse of the Fox's wedding.

They say, there was one boy whose parents
were careless – arguing or in passionate embrace
a stolen moment – they left him to wander
and he saw it all: the Fox with his coal black eyes
and red grin; the Bride in her green dress, the chill
of dread so manifest her footsteps frosted
the new grass. Wonderstruck the boy
followed the sight and noise, the bold flags,
the baying horns, the drums, the drums.

They say, how in the apple orchard the boy
hid behind brambles to watch. He was nabbed,
dragged out, tried and spared after a manner
thanks to the Bride's pleading. 'As she begs,'
said the Fox, 'I'll not rip out your throat.'
And he gave the weeping boy a sideways smile.
'But everyday you'll wish I had not been so kind.'
And he glanced at his Bride as she stood on a patch
of ice-fringed green and stared him down.

They say, an iron knife was placed in the boy's hand,
they spun him thrice, and put him on the path home
though it never felt like home again. The boy lost
first the word for it, then a word a day all that year:
the word for primrose, for comfrey, for stone, oak,
the name of the stream that crossed the muddy lane,
the words for minnow, magpie, mother. At last
he was silent as any beast, and lonely. And
his iron knife, it was the only thing that spoke.

HERMENEUTICS

'I' ends and 'You' begins.
Imagine it is halcyon. Stepping out
of the soft mulch, bound together

as if in a three-legged race.
But then, reaching for her breast
he grasps instead his own knee.

She talks non-stop and her voice
is his own, clattering inside his head.
She broods. Refuses to lie under him;

will only fuck if she is on top. Sulks.
Laughs too loudly. Eats their children.
Is – exhausting. And so, although

it's slow work scraping flesh from bone
at last they peel themselves apart and
she can't get away fast enough. She

scrambles over the wall; sprouts wings.
That night he hears her shout her name
jubilant. Then silence presses down.

Once there was a girl (or boy)
who woke alone in the forest.
Dark as it was s/he set off home
letting feet find path until at last
the path split and there were two.

The first was the path of needles.
A path so sharp in the telling
it slid beneath the skin.
To travel this path is to journey
outside-in; to slip through
the needle's eye small as a flea.
S/he took the path of needles
to ask needle-sharp questions.
To feel with his/her own fingers
along the border's selvedge
the fat, neat seam,
the herringbone stitching.
To wonder when did s/he
come to be in this body?
This place? How did the forest
embroider and annotate them?
What is this electric nerve?
And how does it and
why does it sting?

The second is the path of pins.
On this path s/he collected and
catalogued dreams, spelling
them out in silver pin-heads.

S/he is pricked to ask: what
do I know about this place?
Is this body my own or another's?
Who holds in their hand such a
plump, green pin-cushion?
Who has travelled here before?
Who follows? Whose scissors?
S/he pins a sheet of tissue paper
against the form; pricks an outline;
his/her body (or some other's);
cuts out a pattern and trims it
to the shape of girl/boy
a forest/two paths diverging
the rough, weedy selvedge
sharp needles/silver pins.

THE NEEDLE PRINCE

She finds him lying a little off the path in a thicket of larch & pine,
facedown on the forest floor, his body a-bristle with needles & pins.

She finds him a little off the path. The wink of steel pinches a bite
from the gloom and prickles her eyes. She sees needles & pins.

Face down on the forest floor when first she catches a glimpse.
Thinks he is dead. Thinks the glimmer of needles & pins a trick.

Thinks at first he is dead but nudges him gently with her boot,
then kneels and touches the silver pelt of needles & pins.

They chatter & stir. A pin pricks her finger and with a curse
she tugs it out. Red beads of blood sprinkle the needles & pins.

It will take her three days & nights to pluck them from him, one by one.
She wishes some other had found him a little off the path, all needles & pins.

She wishes she had left him face down on the forest floor. But nonetheless
she begins the job, pinching them out, needle by needle & pin by pin.

Through rows of larch & pine the slantwise light stripes gold & green. Sunset. She works by touch from pitch black to first light: needle, pin.

Dawn strikes a spark from the silvered prince. He sighs and needles & pins chatter & sing & tap their heads together. The wind picks up, brings rain.

The pine masts knock & creak. Dusk, the second day, and a fox flinches by. Stops a moment to stare & say, 'Why needles? Why pins?'

'Don't ask me,' she replies. And wishes her sister would come. Wishes her mother could take her place and kneel, nip & lift them out, needle, pin, one & another.

Hears her mother saying, 'Child, I've got this covered.' But still it's just her & him. She remembers on the morning of the third day how this ends with needles & pins.

Looks for helpers – ants, wren, mice – but none appear. Looks at the needle prince and thinks, 'Is he why I stepped off the path? Or is this a trick to make me his wife?'

The slantwise play of light. The silver wink. She stands, dusts off her knees. Turns her back on the silvered prince. Whistles as she walks away from needles & pins.

Describe the box.
> *It is square, carved from elm with a brass hinge and lock.*

I see you hold it in your hands.
> *I hold it against my body, so.*

It is a burden.
> *It is the size of a tea-caddy.*

It is an object of beauty.
> *You could call it beautiful. The grain, the glow.*

The box is very old.
> *The box would prefer we not discuss its age.*

You found the box.
> *Rather, it was where I'd been told it would be.*

And it was locked when you found it.
> *Tight as a nut.*

Why did you unlock the box?
> *Because the key was in my hand.*

You had the key.
> *It was my little finger.*

You had the key.
> *I wore it on a ribbon around my neck.*

Why   why did you open the box?
> *Because the key sprang the lock.*

Does the box belong to you?
> *Certainly.   In my dreams.*

It was yours to open.
> *I did the thing that had to be done.*

Did the box contain what you expected?
> *It held what I needed at that time, in that place.*

No more or less.
> *Yes. I would say that is true.*

And now what is in the box?
> *The box is empty.*
Nothing then.
> *(Silence.)*
Nothing then.
> *I wouldn't say so.*
> *I would not say nothing.*

AND THEN WE SAW THE DAUGHTER OF THE MINOTAUR

She has a big heart, black glass eyes and seven stomachs spooled to a labyrinth beneath the cage of bone and cartilage. You wouldn't think it to see her – hands delicate as luna moths – how tirelessly she chased the thread of herself birthing this or that along the way until the floor was tacky with blood.

Every door is the bitter end. But turn the key and the last door opens back upon the place you set out from. Here again and still so very far from what you're looking for. Why you left home. Why you can't return. She knows. The Minotaur's Daughter is a double-bitted axe cutting both ways.

On the terrace jasmine has taken root through the marble, the vine thick as her wrist and the night-scent bruising. She rises from her seat at the table never mind the children are watching. A dog barks and she nods her horns and scythes your legs from under and you tumble like a shock of corn.

Yes, the universe is a musty old backcloth, moth-nibbled so the flecks of light shine through and you wait in the wings wearing a dress they call diaphanous. Embarrassingly so. But then the band strikes up and in a rush like a spill of milk you see the wheel of suns turning and she folds you under and down you go.

THE HOUSE OPPOSITE

And later, wherever it is you settle
that first house shines through like the lustre
of wood beneath layers of tempera.

The cavernous cellar is long since flooded.
A flight of brick steps ends in a sink of black water.
Shut the door on the dark. Draw a chalk circle.

Here is the attic window framing the moon.
Here is the wardrobe, the bookcase, the stool.
Here a staircase that twists to ladder spanning

root and bloom. It is a bridge blown from glass.
So trot across. At the table three women sit and eat,
look up as you enter, move to make room for one more.

THREE WOMEN AROUND THE TABLE

Bus stop, basket, sunhat and home from the market
with *ñames, cebollas, ajo, huevos*. A pot of peppers
on the doorstep, fat red flames nestled amongst
the green leaves. The room at the back of the house
described as a kitchen/studio/kennel/nursery.

Wednesday lunchtime and they each draw a card –
the Sun, the Wheel of Fortune, Death reversed –
and lay it on the table amongst the yellow corn,
tomatillos and pinto beans.

Remedios shreds cilantro; Kati smashes garlic cloves;
Leonora reads aloud, her words spiced by the anguish
of six rowdy crows stripping the fig tree in the courtyard.

A white crane descends to sip water from
the fountain and the Chihuahua cocks
his leg against a canvas frame. In the margin
of her book Leonora draws a hen wife
in black charcoal. And before it is time
for the children to come home from school
a decade might pass and these three women,
gathered together in the alchemical kitchen,
pressing out tortillas with corn-dusted hands
will see their husbands die; will grow old;
will drink tequila with lime juice from clumsy,
salt-rimmed glasses; will quarrel and sulkily
observe that the coffee is too bitter and black;
will watch moonrise over turquoise mountains;
will listen for owl song; will speak in tongues;
will make each other's portraits; smoke cigars

and gossip; will go outside barefoot to remember
the heat of the day in the cracked pavement;
will make crowns of broken eggshell and eat figs
dipped in honey; will hold hands around the table;
cry as they recall the war, their mothers; doze
in their chairs while the table becomes a rose bush
or a circle of black earth planted with blue cabbages.

CABBAGE

Slung from a trug it rumbles across
the kitchen table, this flabby magenta fist
of stalk and leaf, this bundle of pages
flopping loose from their binding
this globe cleaved with a grunt leaning hard
on the blade and I look down on this
confounded universe halved in my hand
shout   'I can believe in the cabbage!'

And yes, lean in to sniff iron and damp earth
prod the pleats packed with butterfly eggs
constellations neat as a convent girl's stitches
this leathery, creased leaf a dish of galaxies
this bloody alchemical rose, this labyrinth
quick, keen I unscrew a jar of condiments
cinnamon sticks, star anise and clove
shout louder   *I believe in the cabbage!*

THE GIANTESS

And on this very day our Giantess   was not hatched (or born)
but emanated god-like in broad brushstrokes feathering the near
    then far horizon
as murky rainclouds gathered and the sky knelt to the sea

Until [*gasp!*] she stood among us, her pale bare feet
planted dainty on the sand hills – guardian of all a day can offer: the
    reaching trees,
the pack of dogs, the timid islands and astonished sea-creatures

What a hoot we thought, this Giantess of the scratchy shoreline,
and her great wisdom and our startled smallness, rushing with all the
    tasks still to do:
spinning, milling, drumming fruit from nubby olive trees

Sure we knew she was trouble, never mind her bright owl-face,
sad eyes and little mouth pursed to say naught but mumble the   *oh! Oh!*
Our Giantess mortified each hour from dawn to dusk

and only the birds tumbling from the creamy folds
of her cloak refused to be surprised. Not by her glassy silence. Not by
    the whales
coasting sea-green alongside our fishing fleet

Nor by the chimera – hazy as a roll of smoke –
which we chased for a day and a night with our dogs and our pitch-forks
    and our holy
terror until the corn was flattened and our children wept

But   she held an egg – speckled as mercy
[*An egg!*] in the cup of her hand! So we knelt, built fires beneath the tent
    of her dress
and doing our best to rouse her   we lifted our voices in song.

III: NIGHT JOURNEYS

ELEGY
i.m. C.E.

Lying flat – because that's where the day
has placed me – I face the ceiling.

A fine crack splits the smooth plaster-
work revealing where the bay window leans

away from the house. Someone says,
'Give me your weight.' And I do. Hands lift

and cradle my left arm, first stirring
the humerus in its bone cup. They

lay my arm at my side and begin
the slow process of speaking to my

mute muscles, fascia, flesh. Gently
kneading. Tapping. Wringing me out.

And it is then I feel her shift.
Folded in the confines of my chest –

downy and white – she stirs, she creaks.
(I know what you'd say about all this:

the snow goose feels like sentiment. Yet
you were the child who knelt to sing *Addio,*

del passato bei sogni ridenti to a schoolfriend.)
Snow goose stretches her long neck. She sighs.

Her coral beak knocks my ribs. Feather-
borne I lift my head. *Farewell,*

she says.

ROSAMUND

Painstakingly
I learn things
you always knew
but did not teach me:

your mother-tongue
how to knit and stitch
plant a garden
lay and light a fire.

From your mother –
the gambler – you learnt
to bluff, conceal your hand,
lay the false trail

I pick over,
a sorry magpie
sounding out words
in barbed Cyrillic –

letters and postcards
sent eighty years ago.
With your sister you
gossiped in Russian:

chortled, rolled words
around your mouth
like oysters. Gulped
them down unbitten.

I eavesdropped.
Relished the tales
you chose to tell me
knotting truth with fiction.

Memories formed
an artless patchwork.
Drawing your quilt
over me at night

I see familiar patterns;
am pricked by a pin
you left stuck
in a crooked seam.

Wonder how many
things I love because
you loved them too.
Plum jam, a new moon,

ploughed fields, fairy tales,
rowan trees. Secretive,
I share your habit
of silence.

Not merciful –
but familiar
like the red scarf
you knitted for my

thirteenth birthday,
soft midwinter wool
red as your cheeks,
recalling your name.

NIHT-SANG

The danger of lying in the dark and dreaming
before sleeping and the words half-forming
like letters scratched on a frosted window-pane

Are we there yet?
Yes, almost there.

and in the dark, half-dreaming, remembering

What is the place we run to?
Just sit tight. Try to sleep now.

when footprints in shimmering snow
are the only trace left of you

Are we there yet?
Just a stone's throw.

see the line of trees hoisting the sky's grey weft

Did you stop and look back?
Once, as we watched and waited

and the wicked cold enters like a shadow
aslant or askew, as a needle etches the skin

What kept you?
I was calling and calling

and the blush of ink and the sparrow's beak
nipping the seams, stitch by stitch,
and the north is a rip you crawl through
to hear the voice that prickles
like frost on a window-pane as you lie in the dark dreaming
before sleeping and the half-formed words leak through.

SIBIR'/Сибирь

North has deep pockets
felt boots, a flash silk scarf.

North is a pest and
stings like a gadfly.

North has a tongue of flame
and knobby, crafty fingers.

North is round
as a malachite egg.

North is a blue note leaning
on the glottalic creak of river-ice.

North is mouthing bone
sound from a Jew's harp.

North tattles like a samovar
her tall-tales steaming.

North is a hut, eaves
shaggy with lichen.

North is a sentry –
Baba Yaga's black goose.

North bangs hard
on a horse-skin drum.

North is a frost-bronzed
wood pile.

North sh-shouts
your name.

The careless lover stumbles against you crying in the stairwell. Below, your sixteenth birthday party comes to a slow boil. He comforts you with a hug that slides down until his hand is on your arse. And in a careless moment you are on your sister's bed, the Hello Kitty duvet ruched under your bare thighs. The clematis rattles dry fingers against the window but he is heavy, determined. And lying under him you remember the steel-toothed rat-trap. Your mother said, 'Don't touch!' but of course you did. You see him again; you like the bite. He fucks you in a nest of bracken on the forest, against the brick wall behind the Stoker's Arms, in the back of his Ford Cortina. He calls her Rusty, another redhead. One night you flinch and he bloodies your nose. The next gives you a moonstone ring and you do not ask how he came by it. He sends you to sweet-talk his dealer; ask for one more week. The careless lover is out when they force the lock and tear the flat apart. You hide in the airing cupboard and remember the fierce leap of the trap as the steel jaws snap. Hear the big man shout, 'Where is she?' Good question, you think, and sit tight.

FIRST DAY (*THAT I OFT REMEMBER...*)

I

Waking – heft of earth beneath her back / its soft scrub at fingertips / the tendrils of plants still incipient / damp / newly made. She turns her hands so palms press down. Wriggles fingers into the warm humus feeling for a way back. Like every new-formed thing / too much / too soon. Wanting to return and

II

A voice / not yet hers / not known to her / tells her: <*No. You will go on.*>

III

Being touched. The brush of air on skin. Specks of warmth. The contrast of cool earth against shoulder, hip. Electric thrill as some small-thing lands on shoulder / tickles its way along arm, elbow, wrist. Opening eyes to a beam of light. A blow. Shutting eyes quickly. Squeezing them tight. Rolling over.
   Thinking: <*I can do that!*>

IV

The bliss / though not yet known as such / of being alone. The buzz in throat and ear of imminence / the rustle of language precipitate on tongue. The bliss / though not yet known as such / of silence.

V

Silence.

VI

The pleasure taken in a world unseen: not described, not communicated, unmediated. The joy of knowing herself only through self / of being unseen / not described / not yet communicated. Of being the object of no one's gaze and

VII

Of living without fear, self-doubt, judgement. Of the garden without / mirroring the garden within. Of being guided by touch, sound, smell, taste. Of experience unmediated by knowledge, assumption, speculation, spectacle, postulation, internal bias, prejudice. Of being immersed. Of being whole. Of being mutable and various. Of being a tunnel of wind. Of being a tree broadly rooted. Of being an ocean / a shoal / a sandbank / Of being without constraints, or boundaries, or gates open / closed, or weapons, or pain, or questions / answers / guilt / shame

The theatrical lover assails you even in sleep with her honeysuckle scent. She keeps you waiting at Stage Door for hours, always late, never mind that you had her called at the Half, the Quarter, the Five. At last she makes her entrance wearing almost-midnight like a cloak. She calls you angel, apprentice, fool. Over her shoulder the moon mutters an apology. The theatrical lover places your hand on her heart. You feel its amplitude, its generous applause the beat of sandalled feet as feverish and unable to sleep you roam the twittens and streets, compelled like a bee to retrace your flight from fair meadow to shadowy wings. At liberty you dance to sip from her lips. Rehearse the starstruck night you scrambled together down the nettled bank and fled, hand in hand, as far as the lake's edge. How you undressed on the damp grass and eased your bodies in, unstitched by silty water. Beneath your feet the gravel bed. You heard the moorhen's oboe-hoot of alarm as you laughed and splashed. Felt pondweed and silver carp brush against your bare legs, and saw the prickle of falling stars as – tuning to concert pitch night's orchestra – the theatrical lover swept up her arms.

SNOW SONG

Spell-bound
By your pale blue eyes –
Snowy singer.

Your name is ice
Twice melted on my tongue,
A symptom or sign

Pointing the way.
A dry cough; a fever
Dream of descent.

I sleep with the window
Open and wake to snow
Feathering the bedspread.

Barefoot over snow-feathers
I go, glancing back
To the blue-eyed singer.

The pond is frozen.
At sunset the ice
Creaks and chimes.

With a long shout,
With a swan's beak, Death
Knocks on the blue door.

I sit up all night and
Your icy hand grips mine –
Dear symptom, dear sign.

We can agree on this:
You hexed me.
You no longer exist.

I've set fire to the ice house.
Snow and ashes fall like feathers.
So do me a favour, singer –

Amen, amen! Melt away like spring
Snow. I will not say your name again.

LETTER FROM SPRING GREEN, WI

My father had fists of steel; my mother had fingers of glass.
I grew up between them, their cub, a paper tiger

crouched on the red Uzbek rug outside my father's study
playing rock, paper, scissors – ice-hearted princess.

I only had to say it once and they hopped to
like sunflower seeds on a hot stove.

The white Kremlin walls were metres thick
and every time they dug to lay a cable or fix a leak

found bones, charred by fire or frost-furred red.
The black earth was thick with them. At night

I heard them rattle and the gold domes
buzzed with forgotten voices.

Now tell me, do I slip and break things
– vases, lamps, clocks and windows –

because I am old, careless and impatient?
Or because I am Stalin's daughter?

They still read my mail and spy on me though
I've long scratched Koba's name from mine. Wisconsin

winter nights are dark and cold. I sit up writing diktats.
Let me go to the movies! Take me to the ballet!

Buy me an ice cream! He wrote back to me
in his wretched, clumsy hand signing himself

*Your humble and unworthy peasant. Kukushka –
little cuckoo – I hear, I obey. It will be done.*

FIELD NOTES, 3

The corresponding lover writes to you on notepaper filched from the munitions factory store. He addresses you *My dearest Angle* – words being a thorny-thicket he tangles with; also misspelling your three-syllable name, the country of your birth, other common or garden words that in his hand snag and turn back upon themselves. But you won't correct him, being truly more Angle than Angel, with your scimitar smile, spill of ink-black hair, and accent catching like a burr on the briskness of received pronunciation. His daily letter names your parts, which he adores: your bumpy nose, tender buttons, how you sing-out his name. He anticipates your next visit; the two of you, hands clasped, creeping in stockinged-feet past the landlady's front room. Upstairs, door closed, his hasty hands are on your thighs and underneath your skirt before you've taken off your coat. Tossing shoes under the bed, jumper wrenched over head, he slides you between sheets grey with coal dust. His fingers span your throat, inscribe your breasts, the round of your stomach and between your thighs, cupping your buttocks. Your body is smoothed by his touch; malleable as memory beneath the press of his thumb. Afterwards you sleep in his narrow bed, the creased sheet an envelope that holds you pressed hip to hip, a near-perfect fit.

NIGHT JOURNEY

At the station's entrance
a narrow woman sleeps. Nested
in rags she has put away
her sign and cup of coins.

Her rough-coated dog
opens one copper-bright eye
but does not lift its head
as I walk by.

Along the track the lamps
rear back against the sky
lift the sheer black tent
mute the moon's light.

All roads are open
on this frosted night.
The rails are crosshatched
by shadow. I walk the way

I'm led as far as the tunnel
then continue until all light
and sense has bled away beyond
a shallow bend in the brick wall.

And now in the dank and dark
I can feel my way, stone by stone
like a child locked out at night
imagining the way back home.

HOMECOMING

My door is stuck. Winter-bloated and
the letterbox choked with leaves. No food
in the pantry, but on the table an apple,

mouse-nibbled. Drinking strong black tea
I take stock: the sharp blades of new grass,
chestnut buds, nettles, red campion

and cow parsley unfurling. The lawn
is shaggy with dandelions and burdock.
I am middle-aged now and these past

six months are the first I've lived alone.
The threads that bind us hardly seem
sufficient for the job, the great distance:

fibre optic cables that shimmer with static,
the lag as our voices boom and blunder
down the line; a pixelated image; these letters

on blue airmail paper; the parcels I send,
bits and pieces to remember me by.
The short letters I receive in reply.

Counting weeks then days. Hours spent
at stations, watching other reunions. Not lonely
just needing to stand among strangers,

to see the jolt of joy on traveller's faces;
a distraction from the hours imagining her,
winter-pale, my bold daughter,

scraping clean the last jar of plum jam
I sent as a sweetening taste of home.
She packed her suitcase weeks ago.

At the station I'll wait on the platform wearing
this old skirt, scuffed brown brogues, my arms
full of hellebore and hyacinth blooms.

You're standing in St Ann's Square. Imagine that.
It is night. Late. The theatre empties after a show.
Crowds, freed from the proclamatory dark, step

into a world dreamt new. Imagine it rained
while they sat inside. Streets left bone-dry
now puddle and glisten underfoot.

Already the clouds have cleared. Above
the streetlamp's reach, the moon has risen.
And stars. Imagine just a few. Spare, cold.

It's yours, the city, in the feckless hours
before dawn. Imagine you have the keys
to every door. They squabble on an iron loop.

Imagine opening the theatre's padlocked iron gate.
Now walk through the wings onto the silent stage.
Stare out across the black yawn of pit and stalls.

The balcony rises sheer, thronged with gilt
velvet, dust. Imagine you walk from the stage
across a park and onto dream-thickened terraced

streets. Pretend you unlock an apple-green door and enter
the house. At the kitchen sink you draw and drink a glass
of tap-water. Imagine – it's after-midnight sweet.

The satisfying lover loses himself in you, spends the whole night looking and finding himself again in stairwells, wardrobes, under the bed. Morning comes and he runs up the stairs, cheeks pinked by frosted air, blue shadows under his eyes. Clambering into your warm bed he makes a tent of linen and eiderdown; presses his mouth to your mouth. You are a millpond. Drawing one sharp breath he dives in; curls and turns against the dark water like a trout. You are a labyrinth. He burns the ball of twine and enters blind. You are a knotted shoelace. He kneels to unpuzzle you. You are the score he sight-reads and he sings you sweetly. And when the door is locked, the window beyond reach? Then he lifts you up, steady as you scale him, foot on his knee, then cupped in his hands. He does not flinch when you grip his shoulders with your toes. Sways and braces himself as you unclasp the latch, push the window wide and step over the sill.

IV: AN EXPLORER'S HANDBOOK

ARRIVALS/DEPARTURES

Someone's daughter, sister, mother
carries two silver coins
and three cakes soaked in honey.

Careful stepping into the boat
not to touch the water because
she wants to remember everything:
where she came from, where she is going.

> Someone's daughter, sister, mother
> sits for hours. Her body succumbs
> to turbulence, to the pitch of motion

> a vibration that lifts her through the clouds.
> Obedient not hungry, she unfolds her table,
> takes a box, peels back the plastic film and
> spoons in the rice, one mouthful, another.

Someone – her name stolen by water
stands as land and sky resolve in shadow.
When they reach the shore dim forms appear

calling *Who? Who? Who?* She brushes past,
jumps clear of the boat onto a strip of gravel,
breaks a sandal strap. Shouldering her bag
she – someone – walks away from the river.

> Someone yawns – pouring through
> time zones. Lifts the window-shade
> to watch the quick charge of nightfall

blue-black sky and a ghosting new moon.
Sees the taillights blinking red, red, red.
She has two passports; one for going
and the other on which to enter.

And holding her sheaf of papers walks
a hall of long shadows, blue strip lighting,
no windows. Not yet the place she set out for

which she has yet to enter, standing
in a crowd of others, comforted
by the heft of her bag leaning
like an old dog against her ankle.

       Someone – reaches the place where she must
       feed Cerberus, throws a honey cake to each
       snarling head then nips through the gate.

       The cavern roof dips as she descends, walking
       on sharp-toothed gravel carrying her sandal
       by its broken strap, dragging her bag. Tunnel
       diverges. She hesitates, tries to remember.

Stands in the press of others. Clutches her two passports.
Hears voices shouting: *You have yet to cross the border.*
For your own security you must wait until called.

This is not an arrival. You are still in transit. Do not use
your phone. Do not do not speak to the person next to you.
She tries to ignore their soft weeping. Remembers
how the heel of her foot touched the water

FOR THEREBY SOME HAVE ENTERTAINED ANGELS

The Ukrainian girl working
a double-shift in the gelateria
knows all about being a stranger
in a strange land.

She has grey eyes and
lemon-yellow hair. Wears black.
Leafs through her dictionary
on the counter as if shuffling
a fat pack of cards. Tells
how to find the thing
my heart most desires:

blood oranges
from the *Sessa* superstore
on the edge of town.

The Ukrainian girl hands me
a creased plastic bag and says
ask everyone, and then
ask and ask again,
show them the address
on this bag until at last
you find your way.

AN EXPLORER'S HANDBOOK
Dodwell, Christina. London: Hodder & Stoughton, 1984.

Obtain a horse. At local markets look for a hardy
independent type, still fat after winter.

Fleet the hours at police roadblocks
by pressing wild flowers, writing letters, mending clothes.

Red ants can be used to pinch-closed a deep cut.
Comfrey is also known as 'knitbone'.

Hunting: you can summon a crocodile by calling
through cupped hands so sweetly, '*Nyark! Nyark!*'

Or flicker your torch across the moon-scaled
river and watch their eyes snap to red.

Birds will lead you to the nearest spring.
A sturdy camel carries 600lbs with ease.

In the Sahara wells may be one-hundred feet deep.
Looking down you see a circle of metal sky.

Bring rope long enough or you will smell
the water, but die of thirst anyway.

The magnetic needle of a broken compass will point
north if placed on a leaf floating in a bowl of water.

Tested exits from tight corners: smile politely, offer
mugs of tea, surprise is the essence of self-defence.

For pre-expedition advice about breakdowns,
what spares to take and how to cope, see Appendix 2.

Breaking camp, leave no trace. To kill a fire beat it,
stamp it out, cover it with earth, water, and sand.

It occurred to me that every day we awoke lost, were lost
as we travelled, and stayed lost all night as we slept.

Here is a doily made by one woman as a gift for another – loved like a sister – who vanished soon after. Barely, she had time to place the round of lace beneath a potted plant, before the tornado lifted her away. Where it dropped her, who knows for sure. Somewhere east and north, beyond the mountains, beyond towns and railways and postal service. Her friend, for all the years of looking, never found her. Now the doily sits under a plant (a plush-leafed violet) on another's table. It has aged to a nicotine-yellow hue: the colour of sea fog, of *Not Known at this Address*, of places that can only be returned to in dreams, transformed yet uncannily familiar. Each tiny knot holds tight, as hands clasp before parting, a fastness against forgetting.

Here is a slipper – one surviving half of a pair – the felt sole slick as mackerel-skin. The crocheted foot is a colour that evokes the linoleum floor of a communal kitchen: of cabbage dumplings, dirty canal water, and the old palace's shrapnel-scarred walls, converted by flimsy partitions into cubicles for living. Having lain for months in the stairwell beneath a pile of rubbish. Having been slept on by a spaniel, carried to a three-sided bed after the loss of her puppies, it smells of that dog's secular and unassailable loyalty. And still the slipper holds the shape of the foot that wore it in the solitary decade of whispered conversations, when husbands and sons were imprisoned, and every attempt at friendship foundered upon those old buffers of self-reproach and loneliness.

Here is a potato peeler – the silver bow that fits the palm, its blade worn thin by paring. When everything else has been sliced away, this it will know: Leningrad, November 1946, and in the Bay of Finland sea-ice forming. At midnight he returns and their conversation takes the shape of the waxing moon; two phone calls, two interruptions, a hard frost but no snowfall. Alone at last they sit across from each other in the unheated room, and can imagine no other place, no other. The shutters are closed. On the back of the door hangs her winter coat, worn at the collar and elbows. She recites a poem, something new, but will not let him put her words to paper. His pen remains capped in his pocket. At 3am they drink a glass of tea and share a dish of boiled potatoes. For all the cold and dark, through their talk she has a sense of daylight breaching.

THE EARLY MEDIEVAL BALKANS

The old map confounds.
A finger tracing boundaries
mistakes borders for rivers and roads
a tea-stain for a pearly lake or estuary
and an ink-fleck for a walled town.
Always someone going somewhere
in a tremendous hurry: call them
Bulgars or Avars or Ostrogoths.
Listen for steppe-sure hoofs
treading the silk road to dust.

Lost in the woods northwest of Cluj
the envoi, asleep in his saddle, dreams
of wrestling a bear. He sways in its arms
a rough-ready polka. And wakes to the tune
of east-wind scraping against conifers.
The letter, *null cipher*, ticks inside his satchel.
He's in love with a woman whose tongue
he does not speak. There are three sides to this love –
her, him, war – pacing out the miles between them.
Blood flows like water and

the river has not yet reached the sea.
A week later and the eastern sky
is black with smoke and crows.
In the musty, cluttered gatehouse
a middle-aged man struggles
to fasten the fibula
of a tarnished breast-plate.
The buckle won't bite down
on the leather strap. He thinks,
This fit perfectly the last time I tried it on.

A GREAT WORK

What stirs the blood?
Not tea and muffins.
Not tatting and quilling.
I like to wrestle. I like the heavy lifting
the hard work of shaping and making
as the sea at Cooden Beach relishes
the work of lifting the shingle
across its own threshold.

I love you because loving you
is not light work, not woman's work.
Yet it is the patch I have been given.
Clay and sandstone hefted by the shovelful
clearing a space on rough ground
for something to take shape.
It is not dainty work but a shift
to suit this grafter's love.

One day I woke to find my heart
had upped sticks and gone east
like the village of Russian serfs
you spoke of: fugitives, unwavering
in their belief in some distant place –
the underground kingdom of Belovodye
ruled by the White Tsar and the Maiden Truth
where each person gains, at last, the thing she longs for.

Two steamer trunks; a satchel of books; a thousand rouble note; five boxes of tinned sardines, black and white bread, Chinese tea, sugar, forty pounds of plum pudding; two dozen boxes of oil-lamp wicks; Jæger flannel undergarments; a pair of long-haired stockings; a letter of introduction from the Empress Maria Feodorovna; a thickly wadded eider-down ulster; a full-length sheepskin coat; a reindeer-skin coat; a pair of gentlemen's hunting stockings; mittens; felt boots; a fur-lined cap; the et-ceteras of shawls, rugs, and blankets; a map; my father's compass; a travelling companion (Miss Ada Field); a whip and a revolver;   a sledge; a Cossack driver; a bottle of vodka;   a *troika*;   a pack of dogs;
          nightfall;   a frozen lake;

              a forest;

                              a road.

ON SLEDGE AND HORSEBACK TO OUTCAST SIBERIAN LEPERS
Marsden, Kate. London: The Record Press, 1892.

To her most Gracious and Imperial Majesty
THE QUEEN
This story
Of a woman's work
On behalf of helpless, hopeless, and homeless outcasts,
is,
Dedicated.

Chapter 1
The writer's object – The herb, reputed to arrest the progress of leprosy –
Arrival in Moscow – The Golden-Headed City – Taken for a spy –
Mounting the sledge – Off!

Chapter 2
The pleasures of sledging along a broken road – Wolves – A cheap 'hotel' –
Roses in Siberia – Pirate drivers – A petition to the Empress –
A feather bed at last.

Chapter 3
Mostly mishaps – Russian harness – Minor inconveniences –
We are shot onto a river – A smash – Those horses! –
Convicts travelling in winter – A pitiable sight.

Chapter 4
Clanking chains – Omsk hospital and prison – Free dinners for the poor –
Scene in an étape – Deserted! – Haunted dreams –
Dangers of crossing thawing rivers.

Chapter 7
Area and population of Yakutsk – Native traits and habits –
Rules of etiquette – Laying up stores for twelve months – My outfit –
A wise dog – The start of the 2000 miles' ride on horseback.

Chapter 8
What the map says – Sinking into bogs – Visions of home – Bear alarms –
Graves with a tragic history – A very simple breakfast – Keeping my journal –
Depression – Arrival at Viluisk.

Chapter 11
Stumbling onwards – Forest solitude and the screech of owls –
A witch fable – The earth in flames – Picking our way through fire –
A mad horse and a narrow escape – In God's hands – Exhausted.

MUCH TO MY REGRET

Under the birch-wood table we hold hands tapping
fingers against palms in make-believe semaphore
trying this tune or that, toying with secrets.

The samovar sings.
Our host – a creased old woman –
believes it has a soul.

Steam rises like the stories we tell
snug by the stove whilst outside snow falls
rivers freeze and winter shackles itself to the land.

Our driver says at last the roads and rivers
are hard as iron and the way east is clear.
He bows to the red corner and prays.

Dressed for a long journey my dear friend
lumbers about the room cocooned
in layers of silk flannel wool felt and fur.

I look to the candle on the table.
The guttering flame leans into the horn shield
as I would lean into her hidden places
wanting what she will not allow me to have.

        'Father requires my return to Chiswick,'
she says
folding the pages of a letter
the means of her summoning
though our mail has not followed us
so very far from home.

She has carried this ruse
all along the *Trakt* of bones
from St Petersburg to Omsk.

The old woman sees my tears.
　　　Calls out, 'What now my dove?'

Ada does not cry.
　　　Snaps shut
her carpetbag.
　　　Shivers.
　　　Says,
　　　　　　'Yes, love, I must go.'

17 March 1913

Reading the letter I remember playing
a childhood game: rock, paper, scissors.
And how I learned from my sisters
that paper cuts and words bruise.

Private & confidential – in an unfamiliar hand.
I burn the envelope and the letter.
Breath comes short, heart banging.
Walk to Cooden Beach walking close
to the sea as I dare, so the rumble of surf
dragging shingle echoes my pulse.
But even the bellicose roar of waves
cannot drown out the words.
Instead, like the long lines of rollers
on and on they come and I am afraid
they will drag me under.

I hear the words chime with the knock
of my heels as I walk home. The house
is dark. If I tidy, yes, I'll tidy this cabinet
of coral, shells, and molluscs.
I line them up, pinked and cream
and hold the conch's freckled, glassy
lips against my ear for the shush
of my dead sisters' voices.

19 March 1913

The doorbell shrills. My dear friend
Miss Norris startles, drops her Conté crayon
and smudges the picture she is working on.
One of the pastel paintings for which, in Bexhill,
she is quite famous. From an exhibition catalogue:
Sunrise Over Sea – Light at Evening Tide –
A Grey Morning – Storm Clouds.
They did not sell as we hoped.
I lay down my book. On the hall table
another letter.

4 April 1913

It takes me fifteen long days
to reply to my accusers.
These things are written: I am
a person of commanding influence.
I am not a suitable person. I am
a terrible fraud who makes a comfortable
living out of the leper business.
I am unwomanly.
But here – my book – a published account
of my travels on sledge and horseback.
Also serialised in the *Girl's Own Paper*.
Anyone can find and read these things.
Or see this attaché full of official papers:
introductions to and commendations
from the governors of great provinces
and other persons of authority:
Her High Countess Tolstoi; Gregory Eremeieff;
letters from grateful lepers; and from my guide,

Serge Michailovich Petroff, attesting
to the résumé of my journey to Yakutsk.
And still they say I am a great mystery
and they say I threw myself upon a simple
gentlewomen – Miss Elizabeth Norris –
the daughter of a clergyman.
They say she seems mesmerised
                    by me.

6 April 1913

The doorbells rings. Neither I nor
Miss Norris move to answer it or
to collect the mail. We sit, silent
and both feign work, absorbed
in the task of ignoring the creamy
white envelope on the mahogany table
addressed to me. In the top left corner
the words *Private & confidential*, written
in a hand now quite familiar.

The letter lies until after dinner.
The maid heads home and Lisbet
– red-eyed all evening –
goes to the hall, locks the door
and brings me the letter.
She places it on the table
beside my chair. I ignore it
and continue reading.
Lisbet sharpens pencils
between fits of weeping.
After a half hour I say
goodnight, very sweetly

and go to my room. And then
when I'm sure she is sleeping
I go back downstairs.

As I write my reply the pen-nib
sticks and stammers a flurry
of black ink across the paper.
I write like it is sword play.
I parry and lunge and each
letter makes a fierce mark
or bold counter-stroke.
I write as if this furious riposte
will appease the wagging tongues.
As if I believed there was a speck
of hope, though I know there's none.
The viper of scandal is still my own
dear friend, his green scales
lustrous after all these years.
I hear the clamour of those
accusatory voices: I am not
a suitable person. I am
unwomanly. I am a great
mystery and I threw myself
upon a simple gentlewomen
– Miss Elizabeth Norris –
She is mesmerised
                    by me.

Pushing open the window I lean
into the fading dark; listen for birdsong
and the boom of the spring tide, incoming;
listen for the shrill of my dead sisters' voices
singing as we used to, in close-harmony.

And what else would you have me do
with my big, rough-made heart?
This heart that trots ahead, teeth bared.
This heart for which anything was possible
but nothing likely. This heart I fear
will one night explode like a meteor
over the Siberian *taiga* making matchsticks
of forest trees and burning bright enough
to be seen from the Bexhill shore. Where
can this heart go and / respectably / and / quietly
live out its days?

Awaiting your reply I remain,
Kate Marsden

BEYOND SIBERIA
Dodwell, Christina. London: Hodder & Stoughton, 1993.

The moment you sit on a sled the dogs bound forward.
Kamchatka – remote as the moon.

Land of permafrost and volcanoes. Reindeer, gulags
and gold. Snow lies on the ground 'til June.

Wearing a deerskin *kurlanka* and three pairs of trousers,
Damart fleece and Gore-tex weather proof.

Also two pairs of socks, gloves and mittens, balaclava,
scarf and fur hat. And I was sometimes cold.

Vitali and I went looking for winter dens, up a broad valley.
Myth says that hibernating bears can read people's thoughts.

It was a glorious day. The sun had a halo, almost a rainbow. Already
minus 40° centigrade according to my travel thermometer.

At this temperature your breath can freeze as you exhale. Tiny
crystals which drop to the ground – 'the whispering of stars'.

Three huts among trees at the frozen river's edge. Dogs barked.
Suzviy scraped deerskin – her scraper blue obsidian set in wood.

I climbed a hill and looked down on the river's course, frozen ox-bow
lakes, sled tracks, fishing holes, sea-ice cracking into giant plates.

Before I reached the track I heard a sled and a man singing
with the full force of his deep, bass voice. The valley reverberated.

A team of dogs came bowling round the corner, their master
wearing a big red fox-fur hat and singing with all his might.

Six swans were calling musically as they flew the river's course.
At night I listened to the clicking of hooves as the reindeer herd

moved around our camp. We made nettle soup, lunched ravenously
on wild garlic, caviar and bread. I felt inexplicably content.

THE STONE FLOWER

Uncut, the block
stays dumb
She sets to work

carving a shape
with fingers and thumbs
Work that can never

be quite finished
Polish smooth
and rub, rub, rub

until the form
comes through
A cup? Bell? Flower?

A flower then
hewn from
green stone

petals revealed
by the chisel's tip
Pistil, stigma, stamen

unfurling from the
point. Malachite
stem uncoiling

Making this
stone flower
and it's one

damn thing
after another
the door bell

the child
tired or hungry
begging for stories

Her hands always
busy with soothing
baking, and folding

On the day's
threshold she wakes
to take up

hammer and chisel
At her bench
the memory

of touch
Stone sings to
the lathe's tune

And the flower
lifts its head
sparked to life

in a flurry of knocks
and chips, blows
and bruises

ACKNOWLEDGEMENTS

The poems 'Dark Peak' and 'Llyn Ddu/Black Lake/Lindow' were commissioned by the poet and archeologist Dr Melanie Giles for the anthologies *Vestiges: The Past in the Peaks* and *PEAT*.

'And then we saw the daughter of the minotaur', 'The House Opposite', 'Three Women Around the Table', 'Cabbage', and 'The Giantess' all take their titles from, and refer to, paintings by the Lancashire-born Mexican surrealist artist Leonora Carrington.

'Snow Song' is a reworking of a fragment of Marina Tsvetaeva's 'Poems for Blok'/Стихи к Блоку. I am grateful to the John Rylands Library and Jessica Smith for access to Elaine Feinstein's Carcanet Press archive, where the drafts of Feinstein's collaborations with Angela Livingstone can be found, and upon which I drew for my poem.

'An Explorer's Handbook' and 'Beyond Siberia' are found poems using as their source two books by the British writer Christina Dodwell, FRGS. I am hugely grateful to Christina for her permission to publish these poems.

'Kate Marsden Leaves Moscow' and 'On Sledge and Horseback to Outcast Siberian Lepers' are also found poems, based on a book by the Victorian nurse and explorer, Kate Marsden. Her epic account of travelling in Siberia in search of a cure for leprosy was first published in London by the Record Press in 1892. The 'Appendix to Official Papers and Letters', draws upon Kate Marsden's letters, held within the Bexhill Museum archive. I am grateful to the Museum for granting me access to this material.

The Emma Press published several of the poems in this collection in my debut pamphlet, *The Fox's Wedding*. I am enormously grateful to Emma Dai'an Wright for selecting and editing the pamphlet, and to Reena Makwana for her beautiful illustrations.

I am grateful for the support of the following publications and anthologies in which these poems have appeared: *Agenda, Aesthetica Creative Writing Anthology, Antiphon, The Clearing, Magma Poetry, New Poetries VIII, The Next Review, PN Review, Rialto,* and *Smokestack.*

Thanks to the Manchester Museum, where I was writer-in-residence in 2014-15; the John Rylands Library, where I was artist-in-residence in 2019-2020; and the University of Manchester's Centre for New Writing, where this collection first began to take shape.

Grateful thanks to my editor, John McAuliffe, and to Michael Schmidt and all at Carcanet for their dedication and tireless passion for poetry. And thanks also to those who helped to make and shape this collection including: Vona Groarke and Carol Mavor; Siân Thomas and Johnny Marsh; Fatema Abdoolcarim, Alice Butler, Suzanne Holland, Usma Malik, Terri Mullholland, Kathryn Pallant, Stephen Plaice, Tabitha Tarran, Jenny Walters, and Mariah Whelan. Finally, I acknowledge with immense gratitude the encouragement and support of my partner, Stephen Wells, my family, and the many friends, colleagues, and collaborators who have travelled alongside me over the years. And Cuyler Etheredge—you were there when I first ventured into the forest of writing offering support and inspiration, and continue to *touch me like the delayed rays of a star.*

Cordate leaves
lie snug
to the bud

Little frills nicked
on the petal prick
fingers and thumbs

Words are good
she says, but
touch is better

There – and she
brushes off the dust
Almost done